# Critical Thinking
# for Social Work

# Critical Thinking
# for Social Work

## KEITH BROWN
## LYNNE RUTTER

Series Editor: Keith Brown

LearningMatters

First published in 2006 by Learning Matters Ltd.

*British Library Cataloguing in Publication Data*
A CIP record for this book is available from the British Library.

ISBN-13: 978 1 84445 049 7
ISBN-10: 1 84445 049 X


Cover and text design by Code 5 Design Associates Ltd
Project Management by Deer Park Productions
Typeset by Pantek Arts Ltd, Maidstone, Kent
Printed and bound in Great Britain by Bell & Bain Ltd, Glasgow

Learning Matters Ltd
33 Southernhay East
Exeter EX1 1NX
Tel: 01392 215560

# Contents

# About the Authors

**Keith Brown**
Head of Post Qualifying Social Work
Institute of Health and Community Studies
Bournemouth University
Royal London House
Christchurch Road
Bournemouth
BH1 3LT
Tel: 01202 964765
Fax: 01202 962025
E-mail: kbrown@bournemouth.ac.uk

Keith holds professional qualifications in nursing, social work and teaching, and academic qualifications in nursing, social work and management. He has worked in the education and training field for over 20 years, working for three universities and three local authority social work departments. Currently he is the Head of Post Qualifying Social Work at Bournemouth University.

**Lynne Rutter**
Lecturer
Institute of Health and Community Studies
Bournemouth University
Royal London House
Christchurch Road
Bournemouth
BH1 3LT
Tel: 01202 962019
E-mail: lrutter@bournemouth.ac.uk

Lynne holds academic and professional qualifications in librarianship and education. Currently she delivers critical thinking, information literacy and study skills support via workshops, tutorials, web pages and printed teaching materials. Lynne has recently completed an MA in Academic Practice and is continuing to research the role of reflective learning within PQSW education.

# Foreword to Post Qualifying Social Work Series

All the texts in the Post Qualifying Social Work Series have been written by people with a passion for excellence in social work practice. They are primarily written for social workers who are undertaking Post Qualifying Social Work Awards; however they are clearly of value to any social worker who wants to consider up to date social work practice issues.

They are also of value to social work students as they are written to inform, inspire and develop social work practice.

All the authors have a connection with the Centre for Post Qualifying Social Work, and as a Centre we are all committed to raising the profile of the social work profession. As a Centre we trust you find this text of real value to your social work practice, and that this in turn has a real impact on the service that users and carers receive.

Keith Brown
*Series Editor*
*Centre for Post Qualifying Social Work*

# Foreword

At the time of writing this text, we are aware of the impending change to the Post Qualifying Social Work structure with the introduction in 2007 of the Specialist, Higher Specialist and the Advanced Post Qualifying Social Work Awards. However, whatever the change that lies ahead there will still be, at the heart of the structure, a need for social workers to critically reflect on their practice. Thus we hope, and sincerely believe, that this text will remain valuable to social workers who want to develop their critical thinking and analysis skills.

This text, *Critical Thinking – A Guide to Enhancing Reflection, Learning and Writing for Social Work*, is one of a series of texts written by experienced social work educators and practitioners working at the Centre for Post Qualifying Social Work at Bournemouth University.

All the texts are written with the specific aim of supporting social workers who are studying for Post Qualifying Social Work Awards in their chosen field of practice/specialism. However, much of the content of each text is also valuable to students on pre-qualifying social work programmes.

As members of the Centre for Post Qualifying Social Work, we all work with the aim of promoting the best social work practice for the sake of all service users and their carers.

I think that you will find this text of good value in your social work career.

Keith Brown
*Head of the Centre for Post Qualifying Social Work*

Lynne Rutter
*Lecturer*

# Introduction

This handbook has been written to provide help and guidance for engaging in critical thinking within the framework of Post Qualifying Social Work (PQSW) education but it will also be of value to all social work students. The handbook takes a pragmatic look at a range of ideas associated with critical thinking, particularly those linked with learning and development.

Critical thinking as a process can appear formal and academic, something far removed from everyday life where decisions have to be taken quickly in less than ideal conditions. It is therefore unhelpful to present critical thinking as a linear process or a set of techniques for everyday working conditions because we rarely have the time or opportunity to follow a strict order in our thinking. We have adopted a more holistic approach and therefore this work does not aim to be a textbook on critical thinking skills. Rather it aims to be a guide and resource to help you to critically reflect and analyse your practice with helpful insight and tips on how to demonstrate your abilities and competence.

A recent review (Phillips and Bond, 2004) found four different conceptions for critical thinking:

- as a generic skill;
- as an embedded skill;
- as a component of lifelong learning;
- for critical being.

All these notions are apparent within the circumstances and requirements of the PQSW Programme. As PQSW and social work students you require a set of initial generic and subject-specific critical techniques to work with, but developing critical abilities within the social work arena can also enhance learning and development and there is potential to progress your own style of critical professional thinking. Our concept encompasses the idea that critical thinking can be developed and embedded within exiting practice abilities in order for a practitioner to deal confidently with an uncertain and ever-changing world.

Our ideas have been developed from practice experience with students over many years and from our ongoing research and reading on the subject. In order not to interrupt the flow of ideas or detract from the informal style of this guide, we have kept referencing to a minimum. However, we fully acknowledge the ideas of others by the inclusion of all those influencing our work in the bibliography at the end.

# Who is this handbook aimed at?

It is aimed primarily at PQSW students who are either returning to higher education after a long break or entering higher education for the first time. However, anyone undertaking the PQSW award or the social work degree may find it useful.

# How can the handbook help with PQSW study?

It is worth considering the purpose of the PQSW award and what it hopes to achieve. As we know the PQSW award is a professional qualification linked to the academic require-ments of higher education and is the equivalent standard of a final-year honours degree. Qualities such as working in complex situations, exercising powers and responsibilities, managing risk and making informed decisions are not only PQSW competencies but also abilities expected of final-year degree students. All these qualities involve various aspects associated with critical thinking, for example reflection and sound deliberation. Critical thinking also enables the application and development of knowledge and skills in the workplace. It can help students extract and express in writing the learning and profes-sional development occurring throughout the award.

# How can the handbook help with practice?

Social work as a profession has always demanded critical abilities and qualities from its practitioners because decisions have to be made 'on the spot' and under pressure. With practice situations being so complex the consequences of any decisions and action are extremely important. The practitioner is working with uncertainty, risk, diversity and differ-ence in a way that recognises oppression, and works to empower and promote the needs and rights of users and carers. This requirement goes beyond 'competent practice' and demands 'critical practice' (Adams et al, 2002) and the development of 'critical being', i.e. a person who not only reflects critically on knowledge but also develops their powers of critical self-reflection and critical action (Barnett, 1997).

No matter what we do we cannot escape our thinking but it can often be left unquestioned in our busy lives. We suggest that developing critical thinking can ensure that we use the best thinking we are capable of in any set of circumstances and apply it in practice.

# Continuing professional development and lifelong learning

Rolfe et al (2001) show that developing practice and learning cannot be separated. The development of practice is a lifelong activity, it generates experiential knowledge and so to practise is also to learn. The most important learning, however, is meta-learning – that is learning about how you learn – and this is the basis of lifelong learning. This handbook also focuses on learning as an end in itself, to develop your own ideas and make critical thinking and practice your way of being.

# Structure of the handbook

In the first chapter we look at a useful conception of critical thinking as a set of 'requisite intellectual resources' (Bailin *et al*, 1999). These generic resources are explored further in the following chapters and are enhanced with more context-specific critical abilities, qualities and approaches appropriate for the PQSW Programme, and post-qualifying practice. The handbook focuses in turn on learning, critical reflection, writing and, lastly, critical practice itself.

This handbook aims to present a number of ideas which should assist you in initially developing your knowledge and abilities on the programme. You are all unique learners and practitioners working in very different professional contexts so we have included a number of questions and activities to help you develop your own ideas and perspectives on this material. If you wish to enhance your understanding further in a particular area you will find suggested titles for further reading provided at the end of each chapter.

# Chapter 1
## Critical thinking

**ACHIEVING POST QUALIFYING SOCIAL WORK AWARDS**

This chapter will help you to meet the following National Occupational Standards for Social Work:

- Key role 5: unit 14: Manage and be accountable for your own work
- Key role 6: unit 20: Manage complex ethical issues, dilemmas and conflicts

If you are a registered social worker, this chapter will also assist you to evidence post-registration training and learning. It relates to the national post-qualifying framework for social work education and training in particular the national criteria at the *specialist* level, in particular;

ii) Think critically about their own practice in the context of the GSCC *Codes of Practice*, national and international codes of professional ethics and the principles of diversity, equality and social inclusion in a wide range of situations, including those associated with inter-agency and inter-professional work

Aspects of critical thinking are apparent when you consider, deliberate, assess, make decisions and discuss or debate issues with others, so most social workers have plenty of skills and experience to build on. We are therefore not aiming to teach or present a set of separate techniques but to start you working with some relevant, generic ideas and principles which can develop your own style of critical thinking further.

We do not intend to cover the full range of critical thinking 'skills' but instead highlight a few basic principles to underpin the process of enhancing the critical aspects of your own learning and development.

## What's it all about?

Brookfield (1987) shows that critical thinking is a lived and creative activity, not an academic pastime.

*Being a critical thinker involves more than cognitive activities such as logical reasoning or scrutinising arguments for assertions unsupported by empirical evidence. Thinking critically involves our recognising the assumptions underlying our beliefs and behaviours. It means we can give justifications for our ideas and actions. Most important, perhaps, it means we try to judge the rationality of these justifications. We can do this by comparing them to a range of varying interpretations and perspectives. We can think through, project, and anticipate the consequences of those actions that are based on these justifications. And we can test the accuracy and rationality of these justifications against some kind of objective analysis of the 'real' world as we understand it.*

(Brookfield, 1987, pp13–14)

Thinking critically can result in major shifts in our ways of thinking and the development of reflective scepticism, i.e. when nothing is regarded as a universal truth or taken on trust anymore. Our assumptions and beliefs, the views of others and existing structures all start to be questioned, no matter what their basis or authority. It is powerful and transformative stuff and the challenge can be extremely positive. However, critical thinking can also be threatening, provoke anxiety and create adverse reactions from other people. It is hard work involving self-doubt and mental blocks, but for many it leads to more creative leaps and insights. If you find yourself being adversely affected by the negative aspects we advise you to seek support.

Critical thinking should not produce cynics but confident people who can be committed to a point of view that is well-informed, rational and supported by relevant and valid material for that situation. These are the type of social workers that the public deserve.

# How can it be achieved?

Because people vary according to their capacities, abilities and experience, how you think critically will be personal to you. To develop this individuality we need an appropriate theory to provide us with valid and useful goals, methods and outcomes, i.e. an underpinning framework and structure. We propose initially to approach the 'how' in our context by using the theory of Bailin *et al* (1999), who suggest that the critical thinker can be thought of in terms of a set of 'requisite intellectual resources'. These ideas have been also been used successfully by Ford *et al* (2004, 2005) in their research on criticality and students in social work education and are explored below:

*The intellectual resources for critical thinking are:*

1. *Background knowledge*

2. *Critical concepts*

3. *Critical thinking standards*

4. *Strategies*

5. *Habits of mind.*

We will look at each of these resources in turn and examine their components, why they are thought to be necessary, and where and how they might be of use. We can also identify those we need to develop further.

# Resource 1: Background knowledge of the situation in question

Bailin *et al* (1999, p290) propose that:

> *...the depth of knowledge, understanding and experience persons have in a particular area of study or practice is a significant determinant of the degree to which they are capable of thinking critically in that area.*

In other words, the more you know about your own situation and the context in which it sits the better. This includes existing concepts, beliefs, values and ways of acting, as well as the usual background information which helps clarify the range of available options, e.g. for assessment purposes. However, professional judgement is required to make an informed decision about the actual use of this material. Thus 'context' plays a significant role in determining what will count as sensible or reasonable application of any standards and principles of critical thinking. This sensitive and moral approach appears well-suited to the social work arena and allows for responsible deliberation.

---

**QUESTIONS**

*You don't know what you don't know, so how do you ensure that you are not missing something important about a practice situation?*

*How do you find out more – who and what are your sources?*

---

# Resource 2: Possession of critical concepts

In order to deliberate responsibly and appraise all the material or information we are presented with, we need to understand the ideas and language (the concepts) associated with critical thinking. This knowledge allows us to distinguish and differentiate among various kinds of arguments, statements and, definitions, and understand how their components fit together. One of the most important areas to consider is our own and other people's arguments (or claims).

### *Basic concepts regarding arguments* (from Gibbs and Gambrill, 1999)
Before we can fully appraise whether someone's argument is valid we first need to know which type of argument it is and secondly have a full understanding regarding the various parts of an argument to make appropriate distinctions and judge whether it is valid.

Arguments are used to suggest the truth or demonstrate the falsity of a particular claim. There are two main types of argument – deductive and inductive.

### Deductive arguments
The appropriate logical sequence for a deductive argument moves from the general to the specific using a number of premises (or reasons) in support of a conclusion or claim. The premises contain all the information in the conclusion. If the argument is a valid one then it is impossible for the premises to be true and the conclusion to be false.

So, if the premises are true then the conclusion is true:

*Premise*: All pilots are people who know airplanes.
*Premise*: All people who know airplanes are born after 1840.
*Conclusion*: All pilots are born after 1840.

Premises will differ in their strength of relevance to a conclusion, in their acceptability/ credibility/relevance, and therefore in their sufficiency to support the conclusion.

However, if one or more of the premises are false then the conclusion will be false:

*Premise*: All tigers are blue.
*Premise*: The animal outside my window is a tiger.
*Conclusion*: The tiger outside my window is blue.

If the premises are true and the conclusion actually ends up being false then the argument is 'invalid':

*Premise*: All fish can swim.
*Premise*: My father can swim.
*Conclusion*: My father is a fish.

How does this happen? This is because in a deductive argument the premises support the conclusion by making various inferences. For a deductive argument to justify its conclusion not only must its premises be true, but the inferences which are then drawn from those premises must also be justifiable. In a deductive argument we infer from the general to the specific. This is where the problem occurs because other factors in a general statement might be present but not acknowledged. In our example we have assumed that it is only fish that swim and so inferred that anything that swims must be a fish. To make it work we should have worded the premise as 'ONLY fish can swim' and then the conclusion would have been valid. But because the premise 'only fish can swim' is untrue, the conclusion is false.

A sound argument is a valid argument with true premises and justifiable and relevant inferences. The problem is that not all conclusions are so obviously false and therefore difficult to spot, and inferences, by their nature, are not made explicit and are usually assumed.

Let's look at a more relevant example Gibbs and Gambrill (1999):

*Premise*: John has an attention-deficit hyperactivity disorder.
*Premise*: This disorder decreases academic performance.
*Premise*: Drug X reduces hyperactivity in school children.
*Conclusion*: If we prescribe drug X for John, his academic performance will improve.

---

**QUESTION**

*What are the inferences here?*

---

**ACTIVITY 1.1**

*Write out a deductive argument using premises and conclusions from a practice example.*

*What are the inferences or assumptions?*

### Inductive arguments

An inductive argument usually argues and infers from the specific to the general, i.e. in the opposite way to a deductive argument. This means that if the premises are true in an inductive argument then it is probable that the conclusion is true, but it might not be. Inductive reasoning consists of inferring from the properties of a sample to the properties of a population as a whole and works with the notion of probabilities.

For example, suppose we have a container containing 1,000 beads. Some of the beads are red and some of the beads are blue. If we take a sample of 100 beads from the container and 50 of them are red and 50 of them are blue, then we could infer inductively that half the beans in the container are red and half are blue. In all probability we are likely to be about right, but we could also be very wrong. Inductive reasoning also depends on the similarity of the sample and the population. The more similar the sample is to the population as a whole, the more reliable will be the inductive inference. No inductive inference is perfect and any of them can fail. So, even though the premises are true, the conclusion might be false. Nonetheless, a good inductive inference will give us reason to believe that the conclusion is probably true.

Many general medical and social work theories are based upon observations of very specific experiments with samples. In our deductive example one of the premises was based on such a theory: 'Drug X reduces hyperactivity in school children'. However, as we know, experiments cannot take into account all circumstances or situations (i.e. the evidence is incomplete). To see if this was an acceptable inductive conclusion in its own right it would be necessary to see whether the experiments with drug X were tested with a sample of children similar to John.

In another childcare context, Bowlby's findings (1951, 1969) suggested that infants who were separated from their mothers at an early age had behavioural and emotional difficulties later. This was used to argue the case against mothers working outside the home. This conclusion no doubt suited the economic conditions at the time; however, the data was based on children in very extreme institutionalised situations and one could argue that these were not 'typical' children. So the conclusion may not have been justified even though the research was accurate. Research usually progresses in this way with later researchers questioning aspects such as whether the sample was representative or whether the research contained assumptions invisible at the time (Cottrell, 2003).

---

*ACTIVITY* **1.2**

> *Do you know of any other social work theories that have been based on inductive reasoning? Why are they considered valid?*

---

## Resource 3: Knowledge of critical thinking standards

Once basic critical ideas and language are understood we need practical methods to help us to criticise something. We need standards that will enable us to deliberate and judge effectively. Standards of critical assessment are specific for each area of activity, i.e. standards for criticising an argument will be different to those used for criticising a piece of research. There are two overlapping aspects to be aware of. Firstly, there are standards that allow us to judge a 'product' itself (e.g. a set of research findings), and secondly there are guiding principles that are relevant to the deliberation or inquiry undertaken to produce the product (e.g. the research methods).

Presented below are the overall standards relevant for the critical appraisal of deductive arguments, inductive arguments, theory and research.

### *Standards for the critical analysis of deductive arguments* (from Gibbs and Gambrill, 1999)

- Does the conclusion have at least one premise in support of it?

- Are all the premises relevant to the truth of the conclusion? A premise is only acceptable if it:
  - is a matter of undisputed common knowledge;
  - can be adequately defended;
  - is the conclusion of another good argument;
  - is an incontrovertible eyewitness testimony;
  - is an unconvertible report from an expert in the field;
  - is different from the conclusion itself;
  - does not contradict the evidence, a well-established claim, a reliable source or other premises in the same argument;
  - is not self-contradictory, linguistically confusing or unintelligible.

- When viewed together do the premises constitute sufficient grounds for the truth of the conclusion, i.e. are strong enough in number, weight and kind? (Small and/or unrepresentative samples or anecdotal evidence would be considered weak.)

- Do the premises provide an effective rebuttal to all reasonable challenges to the argument? This is a good criterion for distinguishing mediocre arguments because many people ignore or hide contrary evidence. Good arguers examine counter-arguments as well as compatible ones.

An argument may be unsound because of the following:

- There may be something wrong with its logical structure.

- It contains 'false' (irrelevant, unacceptable, weak) premises.

- It bases conclusions on too little evidence (generalising from incomplete information) or overlooks alternative conclusions.

### *Standards for the critical analysis of inductive arguments*

- The size of the sample should not be too small to support the conclusion.

- The sample used should not be relevantly different from the population as a whole.

- Any analogies must be valid. For example, it is argued that since A has property P, so also B must have property P. An analogy fails when the two objects, A and B, are different in a way which affects whether they both have property P.

- Important evidence which would undermine an inductive argument should not be excluded from consideration. The requirement that all relevant information be included is called the 'principle of total evidence'.

## *Standards for the critical appraisal of theories* (from **Newman**, *ca* 2000)

- According to this theory, what determines human behaviour?

- What are the major beliefs of the theory – which do I accept and why? Which don't I accept and why?

- Are the assumptions clearly defined, reasonable, ethically and socially consistent with my own and social work's assumptions and values?

- How applicable is the theory across settings, different people and problems?

- Is the theory clear, easy to understand and logical?

- Does the theory address cultural, ethical or racial issues? Is it culturally sensitive?

- What is the empirical (testable) support for the theory?

- Is it original?

- How does the theory compare and contrast with other theoretical approaches?

## *Standards for the critical appraisal of research evidence* (from **Newman**, *ca* 2000)

Look for:

- closeness to truth (validity);

- authority;

- relevance;

- outcomes;

- usefulness (applicability).

This critical appraisal of research evidence requires some specialist training, but these questions will start you off:

- Have the authors clearly explained the purpose of the study, how it was carried out and the results?

- How confident can we be that the study sample is representative of the broader population – or does it relate to my clients?

- Did some people 'drop out' of the study, and if so have the authors accounted for this in their conclusions?

- Have the authors showed how the findings were 'worked out'?

- Have the authors any reason to be biased?

- Are the claims made by the study plausible?

- Does the study add anything to what we already know?
- The main question has to be – can it work in my situation?

# Assumptions and judgement

Generally, we can see that one of the overriding aspects of critical thinking is the questioning and checking of assumptions. To assume something is to accept it without proof. This relates as much to our own assumptions as it does to those of others. A number of questions can start us thinking in a different way, although it is more effective if someone else questions us.

### Standards for the critical appraisal of assumptions
- What reasons/values/attitudes are these ideas/opinions/claims based on? Do they relate to a specific culture or group? Would they relate to others?
- What are the underlying perceptions, judgements?
- Are the ideas/opinions/claims accepted because they confirm what is thought rather than having valid evidence for this situation?
- Which situations do they apply to, and which would they not apply to?

---

### QUESTIONS

*Where do you exercise your critical judgement in the workplace?*

*Which standards or guiding principles do you apply?*

*What assumptions have you come across recently? How did you question them?*

---

### Using judgement
Standards and principles do not always tell a thinker all there is to know about the area they are being applied to or how to apply them because they are generalised from good practice itself. They are not mechanical rules to follow. However, their abstractness gives them a vagueness that makes it necessary for the critical thinker to exercise judgement in interpreting them and determining what they require in any particular case. Which is how it should be if you think about it! The way in which you exercise this judgement and interpret the relevant standards and principles gives you important material for discussion for the PQSW Programme.

Developing such judgement is like learning a language – you don't follow an exact set of rules in speech but you can act in a way the principles prescribe (e.g. using unambiguous words and short sentences) and recognise when your thinking fulfils the relevant standards (e.g. understanding by others, grammar). For example, in practice you may know you made a sound decision by following the right principles (e.g. involving all the relevant stakeholders, finding out background information; challenging your assumptions, etc.) but also by applying the standard that the outcome of the decision actually achieved its goals. The appropriateness of these principles and standards must be evaluated for each particu-

lar context to ensure their validity but it should also be recognised that they will evolve
and change as well.

## Resource 4: Knowledge of strategies, and ways to find things out for oneself

People discover or devise key strategies or procedures for guiding performance in a variety
of thinking tasks, e.g. making lists of pros and cons for decision-making, the use of examples for clarifying terms, discussion with a knowledgeable person. Specific strategies tend
to be more helpful than those designed to apply in all cases. What is most helpful is when
they are shared among people struggling with the same issue.

---

*ACTIVITY* **1.3**

*List some strategies or tips you already have for practice, e.g. making decisions or prob-
lem solving, and for learning, e.g. reading or studying.*

*These ideas are great to share in groups: how can you create an opportunity to share
ideas on your PQSW course – over coffee, via e-mail?*

---

## Resource 5: Habits of mind

As Bailin *et al* (1999, p294) point out, having all the intellectual resources necessary for
critical thinking does not make anyone a critical thinker. The final resource is probably the
most important of them all. We need to have certain commitments, attitudes or habits
(e.g. respect for reason and truth, an open rather than a defensive attitude) and recognise
the value of critical thinking in fostering true belief and responsible action as well. These
attributes are closely tied up with our ethics and values. Social work, with its interdiscipli-
nary nature and its inherent value system guiding judgement and action, is obviously
well-placed for fostering such habits of mind.

In practice we need knowledge about the subject at hand, self-knowledge (recognition of
how we think and reason), plus a range of values, attitudes and dispositions related to
human rights and the dignity and intrinsic worth of all human beings. These attributes
underpin the ability to practise critically and encourage the inherent requirements of social
work: openness, questioning and responsibility.

---

*QUESTIONS*

*Which specific social work (or other practice) values do you think are relevant for criti-
cal thinking?*

---

### *Review*

We have chosen to use one set of critical thinking ideas to develop in this section but you
will probably find other authors' work echoing this material. For example, Smith (1992)
identifies three key factors in critical thinking: knowledge, authority and a willingness to

doubt. 'Knowledge' fits exactly with our first intellectual resource of background knowledge; 'authority' would involve the use of critical concepts, standards and strategies; and 'a willingness to doubt' would be a habit of mind.

As we can see, critical thinking cannot be thought of as something that finds perfect solutions. Rather, the skills of critical thinking allow the best quality decisions or actions possible for the situations we encounter.

---

*ACTIVITY* **1.4**

## Developing critical thinking

*Terms such as 'value', 'empirical', 'conceptual', 'causal' might seem rather academic but they refer to the types of statements used in general speech and when arguing for social care resources. For example:*

*'This child needs help because...:*

- *... he is not in the right type of environment.'*
  A value statement – values are different for everyone.

- *... he has injuries.'*
  An empirical statement – these injuries should be in evidence and are thus verifiable (testable).

- *... he is unhappy.'*
  A conceptual statement – because concepts are ideas that relate to a class of objects they are not specific.

- *... if we leave him he will be subject to more abuse.'*
  A causal statement – assumes one thing affects another.

*We therefore need to be able to recognise and effectively appraise each of these types of statements.*

*You might use our reading list below to find out more or use a search engine like 'Google' (www.google.co.uk) on the Internet for general resources. Just make sure you look at authoritative sources!*

*Social work resources which concentrate on critical evaluation of research include:*

- *Research in Practice – www.rip.org.uk/ and http://ripfa.org.uk*
  *RIP promotes positive outcomes for children and families and for adults through the use of research evidence. Their learning resources concentrate on current research and how to apply it to practice and provide skills development opportunities for improving evidence-informed practice.*

- *Research Mindedness – www.resmind.swap.ac.uk/*
  *Research Mindedness helps students and practitioners of social care and social work make greater and more effective use of research in their studies and in practice.*

---

The PQSW Programme will provide many opportunities to use these critical thinking principles – in applying your new knowledge into practice, in reflecting on learning and practice and when writing. We will now explore each of these areas in turn and develop the notion of critical thinking within each of them for the needs of the PQSW Programme.

**Brookfield, S.** (1987) *Developing critical thinkers*. Buckingham: Open University Press.
A general but insightful look at becoming a critical person.

**Fisher, A.** (2001) *Critical thinking*. An introduction. Cambridge: Cambridge University Press.
Excellent for specific critical thinking concepts and techniques.

**O'Sullivan, T.** (1999) *Decision making in social work*. Basingstoke: Macmillan.
Critical thinking within a specific process.

# Chapter 2
## Learning – applying new knowledge in practice

The PQSW Programme will introduce you to theory and research in the specialist area of your choice. The application of external or theoretical knowledge to practice will usually be an active and important learning experience because such knowledge cannot usually be applied systematically or predictably, and things won't necessarily go according to plan. In other words, it will be a steep learning curve. Developing practice by applying or even just linking new ideas and knowledge is one of the most important ways critical thinking can be practised in the workplace (Argyris and Schön, 1974).

## Applying theory and research

If we look at these processes more closely, we can see that theory and research findings can only inform, they cannot predict or control exactly what will take place. They cannot be taken 'off the shelf' as an unmediated solution or be seen to exactly 'match' a specific situation. In fact, it would be difficult to reduce the complex, uncertain and unstable situations we work with to something that a standardised theoretical body of knowledge or a set of specific research findings can answer (Adams *et al*, 2002). External knowledge will need to be internalised and processed first, i.e. adapted for specific and unique conditions, and integrated with experience and values as well. These 'adaptation' and 'integration' processes can be linked to learning and the development of professional expertise.

The process of adaptation may allow some of the original ideas, rules or procedures to remain relatively intact, but more often they may be interpreted further and then combined and synthesised with other ideas, information and knowledge. This process also aligns with the way we 'learn'. Learning is usually about fitting new material into existing material and involves the processes of abstracting general principles from the new ideas so that they can be matched with, or connected to, the knowledge we already have (Sotto, 1994). Only then is it ready to be transferred effectively to a new situation.

As Race (2001) puts it, the abstracting of principles or generalising involves a lot of 'digesting':

● sorting out what is important;

● extracting fundamental principles;

● discarding what is not important;

● establishing a sense of ownership of it.

There is no model or process for how external knowledge is mediated or generalised to make it relevant and useful – such a transfer of knowledge isn't an exact or linear process, but as practitioners we are constantly building on and using our inputs of information and knowledge whether we are fully aware of it or not. Secker's (1993) work is particularly useful in this area. However, using new knowledge gained from an academic environment for practice is at first conscious and deliberative. There are a number of difficulties. For example, theories and research may be viewed by practitioners as unchallengeable wisdom. To criticise this type of information might seem presumptuous but it is important for professional learners to show how any knowledge meant for practice can be used for specific situations and how it actually 'performs' when used.

From a critical thinking perspective the process of applying new knowledge into practice may require a framework to ensure certain activities are covered which provide the process with a necessary robustness and validity. In other words we are trying to ensure that it is not merely a 'trial and error' exercise. Presented in Table 2.1 is a framework for applying new knowledge into practice with associated general assessment headings for this level of work (QAA, 2001). Such a framework will also help ensure that the process ultimately addresses situation-focused needs, and allows you to demonstrate the criteria on which you are likely to be marked for PQSW-level work.

**Table 2.1** Framework for applying new knowledge into practice with associated assessment headings

| Activities associated with applying new knowledge in practice | General assessment headings |
|---|---|
| A. Understand the practice situation, issue or problem | *Identification, definition, comprehension, diagnosis* |
| B. Identify and judge new and relevant general, underlying principles/elements from external sources for use | *Comprehension, analysis, critical appraisal* |
| C. Combine principles with experience, ideas and values | *Transformation of abstract data and concepts, creativity* |
| D. Design solution and apply to a new situation, or align with a past experience | *Design, creativity, transfer* |
| E. Critically monitor, judge or measure strategy, progress and outcome/s | *Critical evaluation* |

Obviously, this process involves more than a straightforward or linear application of particular technical skills and is a highly reflective experience generating a practitioner's own knowledge for practice. Responsible assessment and deliberation will also be very apparent throughout the process, as well as other more implicit and less conscious elements, for example perceptiveness, interpretation, feeling, reflection. We will deal with the reflective element later in the handbook.

If we revisit our set of 'intellectual resources' for critical thinking in the previous chapter we can see various alignments. Overall, the framework presented here can be seen to provide a number of critical thinking strategies. More specifically, critical thinking concepts and standards would be applied in area B in Table 2.1 to allow the critical appraisal of any theory etc.

---

**QUESTIONS**

*Where else in this framework would critical thinking intellectual resources be used and how?*

---

# Application of practice knowledge

The PQSW Programme will also allow you to explore your own practice in order to show your development. Practice knowledge is learnt and developed from such generalising and application of theories, research, values and experience, etc., and is expressed through professional actions. Unfortunately, many practitioners see their practice knowledge as intuitive and personal and therefore unworthy of acknowledgement in an academic environment.

Practice knowledge does not have to lack the rigour, testability or validity of academic knowledge if we can demonstrate critical awareness, validation and evaluation of it (i.e. critical practice, which will be explored later in the handbook). Eraut (1994) in particular stated that professional education should not ignore the knowledge embedded in application and practice. So much of what happens when we are learning or developing practice knowledge can be haphazard and unplanned. But practice is not always idiosyncratic or necessarily implicit. Whatever is consciously and intentionally performed as practice implies an underpinning set of principles being acted upon. These principles will usually be based upon theoretical knowledge and experience as well as values and are at the heart of the notion of expertise. Argyris and Schön (1974), Schön (1983, 1987) and Eraut (1994) all develop the meaning of practice knowledge further.

The main point is that many of these principles can be explored, and evidenced, by identifying the processes and content of our reasoning and actions. In fact, to be totally unaware of them would be tantamount to not taking responsibility for the effects of our actions, which is unacceptable in any profession. As professional knowledge depends on the range of contexts in which it is used and tested, we can begin to create powerful meanings from our accumulated experience for the purposes of the PQSW award. For many students the process of identifying and articulating their practice knowledge has been a very empowering learning experience.

However, the articulation of our developing practices may prove a challenge to those practitioners who have been out of formal education for a while. Trying to make our learning, experience and knowledge more explicit for the PQSW Programme is a major undertaking. We need to take extra time to examine more closely what we do, why we do it and what this means. One way of dealing with this is to use reflection, which is the subject of the next chapter.

FURTHER READING

**Fisher, T. and Somerton, J.** (2000) Reflection on action: the process of helping social workers to develop their use of theory in practice. *Social Work Education*, 19 (4): 387–401.

**Secker, J.** (1993) *From theory to practice in social work. The development of social work students' practice*. Aldershot: Avebury.

**Watson, F., Burrows, H. and Player, C.** (2002) *Integrating theory and practice in social work education*. London: Jessica Kingsley.

# *Chapter 3*
## Critical reflection

This chapter will help you to meet the following National Occupational Standards for Social Work:

- Key role 5: unit 14: Manage and be accountable for your own work
- Key role 6: unit 19: Work within agreed standards of social work practice and ensure own professional development
- Key role 6: unit 20: Manage complex ethical issues, dilemas and conflicts

If you are a registered social worker, this chapter will also assist you to evidence post-registration training and learning. It relates to the national post-qualifying framework for social work education and training in particular the national criteria at the *specialist* level, in particular;

v) Use reflection and critical analysis to continuously develop and improve their specialist practice, including their practice in interprofessional and inter-agency contexts, drawing systematically, accurately and appropriately on theories, models and relevant up-to-date research.

Critical thinking itself involves a reflective dimension and the idea of reflective learning is therefore closely connected to it (Brookfield, 1987). We may not always be sure about what reflection is (any more than we can fully understand what learning is) and Ixer (1999) in particular argues that we do not know enough about its processes to assess it validly. However, we can understand what it can do within our own context.

The PQSW award assesses the learning and development occurring within educational and practice settings. Being reflective will allow awareness, analysis and evaluation of these educational and practice-based experiences in order to fully realise, and better express, the knowledge gained and the learning and development that took place. The way you do this is a crucial factor in gaining the award.

Emphasis is placed not on a descriptive account of what happened but on a full-scale examination of the hows, whys and what it all means for future practice. In order to do this we would need to reflect deeply and critically upon the experience or situation.

# How do I reflect?

When described in the literature critical reflection is usually referred to as the thinking activities engaged in to critically analyse and evaluate experiences, producing outcomes of new understandings and appreciations of the way we think and operate. The concept of self-awareness is always apparent, which allows the subjective element (feelings and emotions associated with a situation) to be analysed and evaluated at the same time The consideration of external knowledge to provide a broad and current context may also be included.

Schön (1983, 1987) developed ideas around two main types of reflection for practice:

- 'reflection on action' – when we think back on something already done;
- 'reflection in action' – when we think about what we are doing while we are doing it.

The processes involved differ for each type of situation. When we are actively doing something we rarely have the time or opportunity to be consciously deliberative or analytical, and so the manner of our 'reflection' is likely to be much more holistic, intuitive and automatic in the latter situation (Van Manen, 1995), even though we may still take a step back to quickly review what is going on.

For the former situation (reflection on action) we can think of reflection as a developing personal ability. Everyone seems to adopt their own method to help it happen – some people like to keep a journal, others make jottings or notes, some draw pictures or mind maps and others just think in the bath. To do it effectively there are guidelines to follow and deep and critical levels to achieve for the PQSW Programme – these will be explained below. All it takes is an ability to think, to be self-aware and to question – but it takes practice to develop a method suitable for ourselves as we don't always do this automatically. Practice needs time, commitment and some support – these are the variables.

# What does it achieve?

Your reflection will produce a lot of thoughts, ideas, connections and insights into your learning and development. This also follows Schön's (1987) ideas which explore how professional expertise is developed through the use of critical reflection, and also those of Maudsley and Scrivens (2000, p539) who argue that reflection in practice *unites discussion of critical thinking with experiential learning*. Rather than repeating the same experience or implicitly developing one's own implicit 'rules of thumb', etc., a practitioner can explore, understand and justify their practice deliberations, decisions and actions in different ways using critical intellectual resources, and develop new perspectives for future practice using available theory, research, knowledge and experience.

To use the earlier language of Argyris and Schön (1974), we reveal our 'theories-in-use' (the implicit theories that govern our actual behaviour and contain assumptions about self, others and environment) and examine them against our espoused theory (the words we use to convey what we do or what we would like others to think we do) to see if they fit. A small gap between the two might not be a bad thing but if it gets too wide then there is clearly a difficulty. Provided the two remain connected then the gap creates a dynamic for reflection and for dialogue.

However, our need goes beyond being a 'reflective practitioner' in a narrow sense. Because reflection for our purposes is in a social work education context, the main outcome of reflection is seen to be an identification and evaluation of the learning and development pertaining to future practice, i.e. the development of the self as a critical practitioner (Adams *et al*, 2002). The aim is to think beyond the acknowledgement and description of difficult feelings or the elements of a difficult situation to an evaluation of how they were dealt with, i.e. the resulting action.

The overall standards of learning in this context are therefore change and development. These ideas are discussed in more depth by Mezirow *et al* (1990) as the development of practice to oppose and redress power imbalances. The main outcome of critical reflection on practice in a social work context will therefore be an identification and evaluation of that learning and development relevant to values as well as future practice methods.

Argyris and Schön (1974) call it 'double-loop learning' which occurs when an 'error' is detected and corrected in ways that involve the modification of underlying norms, values and objectives, as well as the techniques or strategies. They argue that double-loop learning is necessary if practitioners are to make informed decisions in rapidly changing and often uncertain contexts. This learning should also encompass and, if possible, inform policy changes at the organisational level where appropriate.

# How far do we go with reflection?

Kolb (1984) initially created a model called the experiential learning cycle where the learner changes from an active participant in an experience to a reflector on it then an analyst of it, and then onto an experimenter with new ideas for a new experience. Reflective learning for us goes further to draw out the complete 'learning' for the person and their practice from the experiential process, and links the critical incidents to ideas and theories which shed light on them (Beatty, 2003, cited in Parker, 2004). So being 'reflective' means exploring experiences (positive and negative, small or large) and moving into new understanding. New understanding is a key feature of a deep approach to learning as opposed to surface learning or memorising.

Reflective processes can guide our learning experiences during an event and they can also guide our ability to express or show how this change occurred after the event (Moon, 1999b). Degree-level assignments might ask you to explore your 'reflections' or thoughts before, during and after an experience. As we have already discussed, 'reflection in action' is much more intuitive and so will be much harder to articulate. Finding the time and space to take a step back from an event or adopting 'a helicopter view' over it may help you. Many students have said how reading up on a practice area also helps them clarify their thoughts and conceptualise their own ideas.

The rule is that academic reflection usually has to show knowledge, critical thought, analysis and evaluation. Deeper levels of reflection will therefore gain more marks than shallow ones and we will now explore them in detail.

# Levels of reflection

There are a number of models of reflection that can be followed to develop deeper levels and your choice will be a personal one. There are certain aspects common to most of these models and they have been collated and simplified in the framework shown in Table 3.1, again with the associated general assessment headings (QAA, 2001) to show how they relate to the correct academic level for PQSW work.

Of course it is not possible to regard these levels as totally distinct or mutually exclusive from each other and, as seen before, there are many other more implicit elements not included. However, we can revisit our intellectual resources for critical thinking and note various applications throughout.

---

**QUESTIONS**

*Where do you think critical thinking intellectual resources should be used within these levels and how?*

---

**Table 3.1** Framework of reflective levels with assessment headings

| Key levels and aspects of reflection | General assessment headings |
|---|---|
| *Description*<br>Show awareness of important and relevant aspects of self and the situation – include feelings and thoughts concerning complex issues and dilemmas.<br><br>That is, what, who, when, where? | *Identification, definition* |
| *Critical analysis*<br>Explore parts and reasons, e.g. feelings, actions, decisions, links to literature, etc.<br>Challenge or question underlying assumptions, knowledge, experience, etc.<br><br>That is, how, why? | *Analysis, critical appraisal* |
| *Evaluation*<br>Judge input, deliberations, decisions and outcomes; include ideas, information, knowledge, theory, experience, values, professional powers, risk.<br>Show insight into relevant issues, wider contexts, different perspectives.<br><br>That is, how well...? what about...? | *Evaluation, judgement*<br><br>*Insight, synthesis, creativity* |
| *Learning*<br>Produce and evaluate new understandings, perspectives, creative/original solutions, development, change or learning for practice methods and values.<br><br>That is, what does this mean? | *Development of self and practice knowledge*<br>*Personal responsibility*<br>*Professional competencies* |

In order to understand how the levels interrelate and lead on from one another we will look at an analogy – school science lessons! The way they were written up usually followed a format like this:

---

## Example: Reflection on a science lesson

**The order for the write up**

- **Apparatus**: What did we use? Test tube, Bunsen burner, chemicals.
- **Method**: What did we do? The chemicals were heated in the test tube over the Bunsen burner.
- **Results**: What happened? It went bang!
- **Conclusion**: Why did that happen? The flame was too high.

The apparatus, methods and results sections can be seen to echo the first level of reflection (description), i.e. they are a mere reporting of the facts about what was done and what happened. The experiment's conclusion, an investigation of why the result happened as it did, echoes the second stage of reflection (analysis). This 'uncovering' process would show the teacher how much understanding occurred. For example, did the pupils realise the chemicals reacted differently at different temperatures, etc.?

So this is where the reasons, the issues and factors behind what has happened are thought about in detail, and therefore hopefully uncovered, analysed and explained. It is easy to confuse the reporting of results with an understanding of conclusions. The observational process is important but understanding why something happened, rather than just knowing what happened, is an important stage in learning. However, deeper learning goes beyond this and involves further reflection and investigation.

The next level of reflection (evaluation) can only happen when the previous stage has taken place. In our example we know the flame was too hot and this caused the chemicals to explode but we need to know whether an explosion was our original aim or required outcome. If we did not want an explosion to happen, the outcome is deemed to be 'wrong' and we would want to make sure it didn't happen again. We therefore need to know why the flame was too hot. Further investigation might show that the air regulator on the Bunsen burner got stuck and couldn't be closed at the crucial moment in order to lower the heat of the flame. By looking deeper and enhancing our understanding of the situation we not only know how well we did, we also have new issues to reflect on. We can now use this new information to move onto the final stage.

The last level of reflection (learning) takes us into an area of thinking about the future and into action, i.e. what has been learnt, what does this mean, what changes are needed? In our classroom situation we might think that because the chemicals needed a low temperature it would be important to check the equipment before use next time and ensure the air regulator could be closed. This new understanding and learning would not have occurred without deeper reflection and evaluation of the original outcome.

---

Obviously this is a very simple analogy which does not include important aspects of self, context and values, but it shows how deeper and more critical reflection creates greater understanding and further learning.

---

*ACTIVITY* **3.1**

*Write out one of your own practice experiences using these levels, but try to include some of the aspects we missed, i.e. feelings/self, the wider context, values.*

---

Reflection on some experiences may go even further and change deep and personally held beliefs, assumptions or inner values. If this happens you may need the extra support of someone you trust to help you deal with it, so it is important you recognise this as soon as it starts to happen.

# Can it end up a bit negative?

It can feel negative when things we try in practice don't turn out the way we expect. We can start to feel anxious and defensive when having to think about it all again. But we are dealing with real life and your tutors will actually expect a conflict between prior expectations and experiences. What is required is that this conflict is not ignored or glossed over but explored further in order to develop practice. What is certain is that 'false accounts' of reflection are fairly easy to spot. If you are at all unsure about how much or what you are supposed to 'reveal' then ask your tutors to be as explicit as possible regarding what they are looking for. They should distinguish between what is deemed 'public information' and thus used for assessment and what is personal and private.

Understanding new ideas can involve the reassessment of old perspectives which can be discomforting, whereas exploring the things that have gone right can affirm and help understanding of experience and knowledge in more detail. But reflecting on all types of experiences (the negative and positive) can:

- allow greater awareness and expression of all types of learning and development;
- show enhanced understanding from why things did work as well as why they didn't;
- provide a more positive ending for the negative experiences rather than just leaving things as they were and allow a proper and full recognition of the good experiences and one's strengths.

We also need to understand how to apply or transfer these strengths and work with our talents in new or more difficult situations. We already possess much of what we need to develop but a lot of it lies hidden or unrecognised unless it is reflected on. This idea matches a 'strengths perspective' of social work practice when enabling others. Reflection on problems can weaken confidence to develop in self-reflective ways (Weick *et al*, 1989) but a shift towards possibilities creates new, positive and individual paths for people. Learning to transfer strengths from one setting to another is a key component in lifelong learning.

However, placing oneself at the centre of an event or experience can lead to a preoccupation with the self that can border on self-absorption. To avoid this happening, ensure that your reflection turns outwards as well, i.e. onto practice values, principles, traditions and the wider context relevant to the issue. Also be aware that reflection is not foolproof. Remembering the past is dependent on many different factors and is fallible. When an experience is reflected on, the original event becomes shaped and coloured by that reflection. Many courses advise the keeping of notes or a journal of some sort to record and preserve what actually happened and enable more accurate recall at a later date.

Other useful activities to develop reflection are questioning and sharing thoughts with others, which is why group work and communication with colleagues and fellow students is particularly important on the PQSW Programmes.

## Review

Reflecting deeply and critically is about making sure that all the aspects above are covered, i.e. there is an evaluated outcome or conclusion in terms of *your* understanding and learning and development. These ideas provide the necessary elements to write about in a PQSW assignment but it is important to understand academic writing style in order to articulate ideas in the correct way. The following chapter will elaborate on this.

**FURTHER READING**

**Moon, J.** (1999b) *Reflection in learning and professional development: theory and practice*. London: Kogan Page.

**Rolfe, G., Freshwater, D., and Jasper, M.,** 2001. *Critical reflection for nursing and the helping professions*. Basingstoke: Palgrave.

# Chapter 4
## Writing reflective academic assignments

**ACHIEVING POST QUALIFYING SOCIAL WORK AWARDS**

This chapter will help you to meet the following National Occupational Standards for Social Work:

- Key role 6: unit 18: Research, analyse, evaluate and use current knowledge of best social work practice
- Key role 6: unit 19: Work within agreed standards of social work practice and ensure own professional development

If you are a registered social worker, this chapter will also assist you to evidence post-registration training and learning. It relates to the national post qualifying framework for social work education and training in particular the national criteria at the *specialist* level, in particular;

i)  Meet the relevant academic standards associated with the subject of social work at this level.

This chapter focuses on reflective academic assignments and suggests ways to structure and write them using the guidelines we give our own students. Not all universities adopt this style of assignment for the PQSW Programme, and different institutions will assess reflective assignments in various ways, so it is necessary to check with your tutors before you follow the guidance given here. However, this guidance is based on years of teaching experience and of external assessment, so we feel confident of its value.

In general, the reflective assignment needs to show and evidence practice knowledge, the understanding and application of any theory or research, the learning outcomes achieved and professional development. It is therefore not a description of events or feelings. It should allow your learning derived from your critical thinking and reflection to be expressed.

How you view any assignment will depend on your previous experiences of education, and the length of time since being a formal 'learner', but it will be important not to make any assumptions and to follow your course handbooks and assignment guidelines very carefully.

# Benefits of writing

Academic assessment is dominated by written work. As with most qualifications it is not what you think or do but the way you write about it that is graded. Assignment writing is therefore important because it is a major way in which existing or developing practice can be expressed for assessment purposes. This is a positive aspect because we understand and learn more while we are writing as the process supports and develops reflective and critical abilities. It is also a skill social workers must acquire as it is often via written reports that clients are represented. This cannot be overstated. Good social work often requires the writing of reports for the benefit of the client and well written reports will require the same skills.

According to Moon (1999a), writing:

- forces us to spend the time;

- helps us focus and sift material by slowing us down;

- forces us to organise and clarify our thoughts so we can sequence them;

- gives us a structure;

- gives control – we choose which points to make – and enables identification and prioritising of material;

- helps us to know if we do understand something by attempting to explain it;

- can help develop a deeper understanding of something as we work through it and explain it;

- can record a train of thought and relate it to the past, present and future;

- can initiate new ideas, connections, questions, etc.

Because critical reflection relies so much on making connections and judging our thoughts and information, writing is one of the main activities that can help by starting this process of capturing and expressing basic assumptions, underlying knowledge and the memory of any experience. Writing skills are primarily thinking skills but because writing is slower it can achieve more, especially in developing connections, exploring the experience more deeply and gaining different perspectives.

Writing is not a one-off activity. All writing is about drafting and rewriting. It has a powerful effect in prompting further insights and hunches – the problem is that once we write these down they sound clumsy. This is because these ideas come into our minds as holistic and compacted 'nuggets', so to speak. To convey them in structured language is like trying to translate them from one code into another. It won't happen in one or two attempts unfortunately. Also, this translation process will throw up further ideas as we explore and unravel the original one. It is no wonder we go off on tangents and get lost! The key is to have a structure and a disciplined approach so that we can work with and control all these thoughts and articulate a clear message from them.

We wish to point out here that we believe PQSW assignments need to be based on, and reflect, your practice – hence critical reflection. Society does not need social workers who can write theoretically about practice but cannot practise competently or reflect on their own practice – society needs competent, skilled practitioners. In other words, society needs social workers who can critically reflect on their practice and debate and demonstrate competence. This, therefore, does involves being able to write about it.

## Coverage

Choosing what to write about will obviously depend entirely on what the assignment is for but it will usually be concerned with new knowledge becoming embedded in practice. A study of the assignment content guidelines and learning outcomes will identify all the areas to cover. Then you can decide which experiences or examples will be able to show and evidence these areas best or plan for a new experience to allow this. List the areas the assignment wants you to cover. Then develop some ideas around them. How you do this is up to you – everyone has a different way, whether it's using lists or pictures. But do start – even if it's with 'Once a upon a time…'. Only when something is down on paper or on a PC can you begin to work on it and make it better – if it's stuck in your head it's probably just going to float about doing nothing except worry you!

## Using the reflective levels

As we have seen, reflecting in the PQSW context is about concentrating on the deeper, critical levels, i.e. to ensure that there is an outcome in terms of *your* understanding, evaluation and learning about the education and practice events you are involved with. If we re-examine the reflective levels we can see that the questions associated with each of them can also help develop our initial, often more descriptive, thoughts and reflections onto more analytical and evaluative levels (see Table 4.1).

Table 4.1 Questions to develop descriptive reflection into learning

| Description | Critical analysis | Evaluation | Learning |
|---|---|---|---|
| What did you do? What happened? What did you feel? | How did you do it? Why did you do it that way? Why did you not do it a different way? | How far and in what ways were your goals met? What other factors were apparent? | So what does this mean for future practice and your values? |

We can go further and identify the type of material that might need to be included in answer to these questions at each level (see Table 4.2).

**Table 4.2** Type of material to include at each reflective level

| Description | Critical analysis | Evaluation | Learning |
|---|---|---|---|
| Background | Theory, research | Judgement, measurement of progress and outcome/s | Abstracting general principles |
| Context | Experience, practice knowledge | Strengths, weaknesses, gaps | Insights, ideas, new perspectives |
| Feelings | Values, ethics, conflicts | Counter arguments and theories | Synthesis with existing knowledge |
| Specific relevant details | Aims and objectives | Wider context, other factors | Professional development |
| Definitions | Judgements, assumptions | Different perspectives | Future planning, changes |
| | Decisions,deliberations; reflection 'before, in and after action' | Alternatives | Further theory, research |

Table 4.2 mainly follows a 'reflection-on-action' idea (see Chapter 3 and Schön, 1983) and a linear progression from left to right. It is not meant to be a prescriptive approach and you can use it in any way that helps. However, there is much Table 4.2 cannot account for, i.e. the subtlety, depth, emotion and intuition involved in learning and thinking. Some of the questions or areas may not be relevant to your experience or reflection, and your own individual style and approach may require more holistic guidance to follow.

We are merely suggesting that reflective writing is a developmental and ongoing process requiring time and feedback, and the elements noted above are all important aspects to be included because they are the elements usually being assessed for PQSW level work. At its heart PQSW study is about the demonstration of competence to practice and this cannot occur without reflection on your practice.

# Structure – developing an 'argument'

## Stage 1: Developing a viewpoint and starting to make an argument

The starting point for structuring an assignment of this type is *your* point of view, or your 'claim'. You cannot really start writing a first complete draft until you know what it is you want to say. And you won't know this until all the stages of the reflection process, and initial reading of the subject area, have been achieved. Your viewpoint consists of what has been understood and learnt, plus what this means for your practice and values. It forms the basis of your 'argument'. If you get stuck at this stage use Table 4.1 on 'Questions to develop descriptive reflection' which may help you to reflect deeper. If you still feel lost try discussing with a tutor. Even the smallest practice incidents can be packed with implicit new knowledge or learning but you may not be able see it for yourself without some critical questioning.

Here is a simplified example of a viewpoint:

---

### *Example – assignment for a specialist area of social work: enabling others*

**Stage 1: My viewpoint**

*'Good communication is essential when planning successfully for a placement student.'*

Notes – *I have learnt that because we need people in order to achieve things, communicating effectively helps us achieve more. This is another way we can show respect to others. The literature on placement planning generally agrees. Some authors do not give this area a lot of emphasis though.*

---

## Stage 2: Reasons give the structure a sequence

Once your viewpoint is known, you can then focus any further reflection and research on the pivotal points (e.g. the events or specific instances in your learning experience) which have been instrumental in getting you here, i.e. the reasons behind how you got to this point of view. For a 5,000-word assignment you will probably only be able to focus effectively on three or four main reasons. Too often we pick a subject that is just too big. Focus down – this will give you space to be analytical and not just descriptive. These reasons should be organised in a way that can best persuade your tutors to agree.

By expressing your viewpoint and reasons in this way you are making a claim to knowledge, but this will be viewed as opinion only at this stage by the tutors. In fact, it would also be viewed as opinion if we applied critical thinking standards to such a claim. An experience does not automatically possess an innate validity and would therefore remain merely anecdotal without external connections. You now have to sustain this claim to knowledge in response to (or in anticipation of) a 'challenge' when you are in an academic environment. In other words you now have to show the validity of this view and your commitment to it. This is not unusual, unique or inappropriate – social workers are constantly justifying their decisions and actions when challenged by service users, managers or colleagues in practice.

In this context you back up your viewpoint and reasons by further researching the topic in the literature and offering reliable evidence or examples (either theory, research or possibly other material such as case studies, practice guidance, policy, etc.) in support of your ideas. By showing where this evidence has come from (by citing and referencing it) you can demonstrate its authority and validity for this purpose, in other words apply relevant critical standards to it.

Also look for material that contradicts your opinions to show that you are aware of, and have considered, arguments that are counter to your own. These counter-arguments or evidence will help clarify and sharpen your own ideas and help you demonstrate why they are more convincing. Their use is a good guiding critical principle. If you are applying theory or research to practice we have already shown in Chapter 2 how you can use the literature more directly by critically examining how and why you adapted an idea for your own use, i.e. evaluate its purpose and usefulness.

Achieving an appropriate academic style depends on developing a view of knowledge as 'contextual' (Baxter, Magolda, 1992), – i.e. there are *no* right or wrong answers out there but the knowledge or evidence supporting opinions and views can be constructed, understood and appraised in relation to a particular context or situation. As we have said, there is no absolute 'truth' and your tutor will be assessing your ability to gain an overview of the subject and support a particular position within it.

We can refer back to our viewpoint example and show some reasons for it:

---

### Example – assignment for a specialist area of social work: enabling others

**Stage 1: My viewpoint**

*'Good communication is essential when planning successfully for a placement student.'*

**Stage 2: The reasons why I believe good communication is essential:**

1. *Interpersonal skills (good listening) helped me start the relationship with the student well – empathy, trust being built. Literature on interpersonal communication says these skills are crucial in forming relationships and for education. Dangers to be aware of are becoming too informal and friendly...*

2. *Better forming of communication lines with the university tutor would have enabled better understanding of their role and the ways I needed to liaise with them. I felt intimidated and assumed the tutor would not be available; bureaucracy issues were apparent. Literature on placements says this is a difficult area – need to be proactive. I can discuss ways I could do this better next time...*

3. *Liaison with my team beforehand helped the induction go smoothly – people on side, better prepared. Literature on team co-ordination for a project says that early contact allows problems to surface and be dealt before start. Literature on placement planning says early contact is essential but to also keep overall control by forming clear learning objectives for the student. Discuss links...*

---

### ACTIVITY 4.1

*If such a structure is useful to you, start to develop one for an assignment of your own. Our example was very linear in structure but you can do it using any method you like.*

# Stage 3: Developing points for each reason will make up the paragraphs

Once you have your reasons and the literature, you can then break down each of your reasons into its main points or issues. Paragraphs then raise and develop these particular issues or points using appropriate evidence. Often the first sentence is the key point itself, i.e. it explains what the paragraph is about and contains the main idea. This 'topic sentence' need not come first in the paragraph but it has to be somewhere because it asserts and controls the paragraph's main idea. You can place it in the middle if you have information that needs to precede it. You can put it at the end if you want to your reader to consider your line of reasoning before you declare your main point.

However you do it, the line of reasoning and its evidence should follow and be linked logically within these paragraphs. As you develop the point you tell the reader where you are going with it by making use of the literature, linking back to the reason and the main argument as appropriate. Ideally it is best to sort out one point before moving onto another but if you do need to stop and then return to a point later make sure you tell the reader what you're doing and why.

The next point should always be introduced. Using linking words or 'signposts' helps the reader make the transition from one paragraph or point to the next. There are different ways to do this depending on the way you want to develop your argument. Here are some examples:

- Contrast, or taking a sudden turn in reasoning – 'but...', 'however...', 'on the other hand...', 'although...', 'and yet...'

- Cause and effect – 'therefore...', 'as a result of.. .', 'for this reason...', 'consequently...'

- Sequence – 'following...', 'before...', 'first..., finally...'

- Illustration – 'for example...', 'for instance...', 'such as...', 'in this case...'

- Add weight – 'similarly...', 'in addition...', 'moreover...'

- Conclusion – 'In conclusion...', 'accordingly...', to sum up...'

Returning to our example we can see a specific point being developed for the first reason:

---

### *Example – assignment for a specialist area of social work: enabling others*

**Stage 1: My viewpoint**
*'Good communication is essential when planning successfully for a placement student.'*

**Stage 2: First reason:**
1. *'Interpersonal skills (good listening) helped me start the relationship with the student well – empathy, trust being built.'*

**Stage 3: Particular point/issue to develop for this reason**
This is the point (topic sentence) – *Listening to the student rather than talking at her made our initial meeting a very positive one.*

---

> *Define – 'Listening entails...'*
>
> *Develop – how and why – 'Letting the student speak first not only allowed me an understanding of her unique situation and needs, it also made her feel at ease with me and to start to trust me...'*
>
> *Link to reason/argument – 'Understanding her needs and circumstances informed my planning...; but this conversation also formed a bond between us...'*
>
> *Evidence/connections – 'Bloggs (2003) explains how listening is more important than talking because it shows respect to others...and she responded by...'*
>
> *'Adult learning theory similarly emphasises the need for respect for learners...'*
>
> *Link to next point/paragraph – 'However, the relationship still needs to remain professional...'*

Once your main text is structured you will need an introduction and a conclusion.

# Introductions

We want to emphasise the crucial importance of the introduction. This is probably the most important part of your work in terms of ensuring your writing keeps to task. Don't attempt it until you have a good grip on your argument, reasons and points.

- Set the overall context but also state the main issues you are going to write about and why: it will help you focus and places your 'argument' into a wider picture.
- Point out the limitations and what you are not going to consider.
- Introduce the structure and sequence of your work.

# Conclusions

A conclusion is all too often just a paragraph stuck on the end of the piece of work which either summarises what has come before or gives the result of what happened.

A conclusion offers the chance to do much more than this. It can deliver a concise consideration of the overall *meaning* you have gained from critical thinking and reflection on your practice and/or learning. That is, it can sum up the major issues and points raised from your evaluation of the outcomes and consequences, plus what they may, or will, mean for social work, for your practice or for yourself.

---

**ACTIVITY 4.2**

*Try writing a brief introduction or conclusion for our example assignment.*

---

# Critical style

Developing an appropriate critical style does take time and practice, especially when initial thoughts tend to be very descriptive – here are some more tips. Table 4.3 (Cottrell, 2003, p232) shows how the more normal, descriptive way of writing can be developed into a critical academic style by listing how each element should be enhanced – again we can see similar methods of questioning, delving deeper, assessing and judging things as we do in critical thinking abilities.

**Table 4.3** Descriptive to critical writing (Cottrell, 2003)

| Descriptive writing | Critical analytic writing |
| --- | --- |
| States what happened | Identifies the significance |
| States what something is like | Evaluates (judges the value of) strengths and weaknesses |
| Gives the story so far | Weighs one piece of information against another |
| States the order in which things happened | Makes reasoned judgements |
| Says how to do something | Argues a case according to the evidence |
| Explains what a theory says | Shows why something is relevant or suitable |
| Explains how something works | Indicates why something will work (best) |
| Notes the method used | Indicates whether something is appropriate or suitable |
| Says when something occurred | Identifies why the timing is of importance |
| States the different components | Weighs up the importance of component parts |
| States options | Gives reasons for selecting each option |
| Lists details | Evaluates the relative significance of details |
| Lists in any order | Structures information in order of importance |
| States links between items | Shows the relevance of links between pieces of information |
| Gives information | Draws conclusions |

# Using the literature

As you probably realise, your success very much depends on the type of literature you read (its relevancy and authority) and your understanding of it, *not* how much you read. Quality not quantity! As a practitioner you will also be using contextual information such as legislation, case law, policy and practice guidance documents, as well as theory and research. Your tutor, your reading lists and handouts will direct you to relevant and authoritative literature and you will be looking up more references for any specialist areas, using print and electronic resources.

The particular problem areas associated with using literature are detailed below:

## Making unsubstantiated comments

The biggest single piece of advice given back to students is: 'Do not make unsubstantiated comments, or sweeping generalisations!' In other words, provide the evidence to support your point. This does not mean you never give your point of view, it just means there should be something or someone else to back you up. Here's an example:

> *In my experience I have seen how more effective accounting procedures allow direct allocations of limited fund and enable targeted services to improve. Jones (2004) also shows how services can benefit when enhanced management systems are put in place, especially with reduced resources, even though Smith (2003) had earlier argued that services always became worse after cutbacks. The process of selecting targeted services enabled us to develop our priorities with the service users more positively...*

## Avoiding plagiarism

If you do not say where your evidence or your ideas have come from you will be making claims to knowledge that is not yours (which is plagiarism). Therefore references to evidence in the literature should appear whenever you are mentioning another's ideas, theory, material or research, whether you are directly quoting or summarising them. This has to follow certain academic 'rules' in order to be valid and you should follow the appropriate system as advocated by your academic institution. Bournemouth University uses the Harvard System of Referencing. This can be seen in our examples and Appendix 1 provides further advice.

You can use someone else's work in three main ways:

1. You can mention their theory or idea:

   *The process used incorporated some of the elements of task-centred work (Coulshed, 1991) and systems approach (Payne, 1991; Milner and O'Byrne, 1998) because the ...*

2. You can summarise in your own words what someone else has written, either small sections or overall views:

   *Mrs Jones felt helpless and frustrated at her inability to improve her daughter's situation and appeared to get many colds and coughs during this time which weakened her ability to look after her. Research has shown that those who experience life events that are seen as uncontrollable are more likely to become ill (Stern et al, 2003, cited in Gross, 2004).*

3. You can repeat a small section of what someone has written and place it in quotation marks or indent it:

   *It is not sufficient to be reflective; we also need to use new understandings in our future actions. As Adams et al (2002, p87) point out: 'reflection on its own views the situation unchanged, whereas critical practice is capable of change'.*

Try this method of remembering how to present other people's evidence: Ask – *'Says who?'* and *'So what?'* In other words, say who says this – the opinion and the reference to who said it – and then state why you are telling the reader this – what is your point here? Often we read assignments and case studies and ask ourselves what is the point of the writer telling us that, it just appears to be packaging? Ask yourself, what am I trying to say and why? It will help you to be more focused.

Whichever way you do this, you *must* cite where the work came from in the text itself and provide a reference to the complete work in either a references list or a bibliography at the end of your work. In the Harvard System of Referencing the citation in the text uses the author's last name and year, and the references list or bibliography will be in alphabetical order by author's last name. It is important to look up the rules for your particular institution and become familiar with them. See the Appendix at the end for further referencing help.

## Effective reading

It does take time and practice to develop your reading in order to locate relevant and useful material. Here are a few initial ideas to help you start:

- Reading the literature while you are developing your viewpoint should encompass the wider topic area. Reading once you know your viewpoint will enable you to focus and identify the more relevant pieces of text easily and save you time. Make a note of particular quotes (keep them as short as possible) or paraphrase ideas (summarise in your own words). *Also note the complete reference to the book, journal, etc. at the time!*

- Next, write down a brief explanation of what this means to you – what do you understand it to mean? Do you agree or disagree with it? Why? This becomes easier if you are applying what you read into practice straight away or you have opportunities for discussion about the literature with your peers.

- As we have seen, as you start writing the first draft of your assignment, you will have a good idea of what *you* are trying to say so that when you refer back to these notes you can choose those that are applicable to what you are talking about and integrate them.

## Using 'I'

*NB*: You must check your institution's own rules on this – some universities do not allow the use of the first person in written assignments.

Using the first person 'I' is appropriate for academic reflective writing and for developing personal and professional qualities of self-awareness, reflection, analysis and critique (Hamill, 1999). However, this does not mean the writing should be emotional or subjective (i.e. seen from your viewpoint only). Students who lack experience in writing and who start to use 'I' tend to be too descriptive in their style, e.g. 'I did this…', 'I did that …'. So 'I' has to be used carefully and much care has to be taken to avoid informal or conversational tones within a reflective assignment. Using 'I' should encourage a confident stance, i.e. directness in saying what you mean and the message you are trying to get across. With the addition of the literature, and your viewpoint and reasons, it creates an appropriate academic style.

Here is a short general example from social work to show how it can all come together using the Harvard System of Referencing (from Watson *et al*, 2002, p128):

*I would argue that it is how we as social workers use our legal power in practice that is the crux of developing partnership. That we have legal power does not absolve us of our professional duty to our clients. Jenny and her family members had a right to be treated with respect, openness and honesty (Banks, 1995) in my interventions with them. To me, this included acknowledging to them the impact on their lives that my legal power to intervene to safeguard and promote Jenny's welfare was having. Research indicates that family members stressed the importance of being cared about as people (Thoburn, Lewis and Shemmings, 1995). This extended to identifying and acknowledging areas of Mr Jones's care where he was safeguarding and promoting Jenny's welfare. As Morrison (1996, p136) suggests: 'Partnership is about working with parents and their networks to enable them to carry out the responsibility shared by both the state and parents to promote the welfare of children.'*

# Finishing writing

Check coverage and relevancy – match what you say you will focus on in the introduction against what you have written about in the main body and the conclusion. Also, refer back to your original list of what the assignment has to cover – make sure you have covered all that is asked of you. Ask yourself – 'where have I shown this?'

Think critically about your work before handing it in. Evaluate it using the guidance given here or even try marking it using your institution's assessment criteria.

## *Review*

As we have seen, writing is a process. Each draft will enable you to show areas of learning and development in more structured, explicit and academic ways as you build up a better understanding of what you have done. The main difficulty with writing is to get the real meaning of what you are trying to say past the code of language in which you have to say it.

Each rewrite should allow this by giving you the opportunity to:

- think about and analyse what you want to say more thoroughly;

- reflect on what you have achieved or learnt more deeply;

- read more around the issues and increase your ability to express your understanding of the links to the literature.

By enabling a clear and deeper understanding of learning and practice development the processes of writing should enhance critical practice, which is itself a process of self-enquiry and, at times, transformative change. Our next chapter looks at these ideas more closely.

*FURTHER READING*

**Cottrell, S.** (2003) *The study skills handbook.* Basingstoke: Palgrave Macmillan.

**Watson, F., Burrows, H. and Player, C.** (2002) *Integrating theory and practice in social work education.* London: Jessica Kingsley.

# Chapter 5
## Critical practice

*ACHIEVING POST QUALIFYING SOCIAL WORK AWARDS*

This chapter will help you to meet the following National Occupational Standards for Social Work:

- Key role 5: unit 14: Manage and be accountable for your own work
- Key role 6: Unit 19: Work within agreed standards of social work practice and ensure own professional development
- Key role 6: Unit 20: Mange complex ethical issues, dilemmas and conflicts

If you are a registered social worker, this chapter will also assist you to evidence post-registration training and learning. It relates to the national post-qualifying framework for social work education and training in particular the national criteria at the *specialist* level, in particular;

ii)  Think critically about their own practice in the context of the GSCC *Codes of Practice*, national and international codes of professional ethics and the principles of diversity, equality and social inclusion in a wide range of situations, including those associated with inter-agency and inter-professional work

iii) Consolidate and consistently demonstrate in direct work with users of social care services and/or carers the full range of social work competences across all units of the National Occupational Standards for Social Work and in the context of one area of specialist social work practice.

vii) Work effectively in a context of risk, uncertainty conflict and contradiction

We need practices that allow us to accept and deal with individual and ever-changing situations creatively, rather than make us follow prescriptions. It is therefore useful to consider critical thinking for practice within its widest and most holistic sense as 'being critical' or 'taking a critical stance'. We will take a very pragmatic view and examine work activities to see where critical practice fits already and then look at how they might be enhanced.

First, let's examine how practice can be developed.

## Negative development

On a day-to-day level there are dangers associated with the development of expertise in practice. Any practice can easily fall into purely intuitive and routine methods that are followed because they are safer and less time-consuming. We develop rules of thumb and standardise our approaches to problems in order to survive our workloads. However, these habitual practices are more difficult to keep under critical control, and they tend not to adapt to new circumstances easily.

In these situations uncertain problems may be 'pretended' to be certain, so we can accommodate them within existing practices or our value systems. Or they are simplified by ignoring certain difficult aspects. Matching similarities is easier than acknowledging dissimilarities because they confirm rather than deny our generalisations and so fit our existing knowledge. As human beings we tend to give more credence to viewpoints that are close to our own, and tend to devalue or reject information that conflicts with our previously held beliefs. This saves time and energy and makes us feel less threatened because knowledge relies for its verification on belief, but eventually the process of evaluating our work becomes lost.

However, as we become less subject to dissimilarity and surprise our experiences become non-learning situations as we don't notice what is actually happening. So even though we have more experience in a particular environment we do not automatically acquire more valid knowledge.

The main benefits that our PQSW students report when undertaking the Programme are that it:

- provides reassurance of good practices already being undertaken via discussion with others and use of the literature but also…

- enables them to stop, think and reassess their practices, which allows them to see where they have fallen into pure routine and adopt more appropriate methods and approaches.

Learning new knowledge, talking to others, sharing ideas, applying and connecting them to practice and then reflecting on what happens engages the brain in a different mode. The PQSW Programme can encourage better quality approaches through the content of the curriculum and its assessment, plus allow the opportunity and encouragement to undertake more critical work practices.

However, once the Programme ends the lack of time and opportunity many face in their practice can create barriers to continuing these approaches. The idea of critical practice therefore needs to an embedded part of being a professional social worker (as it should with any profession), with employing organisations playing their full role in developing appropriate cultures and opportunities for it. This is obviously a huge area for debate and concern and may be an issue you will want to discuss or explore further on your Programme.

---

**QUESTIONS**

*How can you deal with a negative workplace culture?*

*Which areas of professionalism are likely to suffer?*

*Are there ways to work round some of them?*

---

# Positive development

We can now look at a more positive model of expert practice and professionalism and see where elements of critical practice can be embedded in a natural way to enhance existing elements rather than become 'add-ons' that are more likely to suffer when workloads rise. The aim of critical reflection is to create doubt and critique of ongoing actions. We therefore cannot undertake it as a set of explicit and separate exercises because it is not possible to act confidently and thoughtfully while doubting oneself at the same time (Van Manen, 1999). We can, however, hope to become implicitly critically reflective and adopt it as a way of being, remaining a positive and confident practitioner. The way to achieve this is to embed criticality within professional and experienced practice itself. But what is professional and experienced practice?

Research by Cust (1995, cited in Macaulay, 2000) and adapted in the list below shows how experienced practitioners (or 'experts' as they call them) encounter new situations.

They:

- *are in control of their thinking* – i.e. aware of, understand, self-direct and self-evaluate it throughout, and…

- *have clusters of 'tacit knowledge'* which form 'patterns' and represent the learning and generalising from previous experiences, from research and theory…

- *recognise other meaningful patterns and principles*, and irrelevant aspects, in a situation and link to these existing known patterns…

- and so *gain an intuitive grasp* of it…

- while *assessing it* in depth…

- in order to *select 'schema'* (patterns or outlines formed in the mind) …

- which when *adapted* to the problem…

- are likely to effectively *represent it* as well as *suggesting a solution* procedure…

- but will periodically *check* to *review and progress and evaluate outcomes*.

Such 'experts' are seen to focus initially on the holistic assessment of a situation rather than on explicit reasoning and analysis. In other words, they have established the necessary intuitive links to bring the different parts of a situation into a meaningful whole, to allow it to make sense for them. Each situation they face may be different but they will recognise enough of the parts to make general sense of the whole in order to start to deal with it. Schön (1983) explained this by stating that experienced practitioners know how to define the nature of the problem or situation first – they can easily 'name and frame' a situation.

Here is one major area where critical thinking can be triggered, usually by recognition of something not 'normal' – possibly an unexpected action or outcome or an intuitive feeling of unease. This is where a critical practitioner acknowledges the difference to a usual pattern rather than ignoring or standardising it. It is where the benefits of keeping up to date in a professional area of practice and having the necessary critical resources come to the fore. Such a practitioner will have more knowledge and awareness to recognise the incident for what it is and have more self-confidence to deal with it explicitly.

---

*ACTIVITY* **1.2**

*Start to link the use of our critical resources (knowledge, critical concepts, standards, strategies, or habits of mind) to the various elements of 'expert' practice seen above.*

---

Good critical thinking in practice will involve appropriate deliberation and reflection almost continuously. In fact all areas of thinking and action need to be under critical control otherwise important aspects may be missed. For example, practitioners may be able to appraise their reasons for a decision but may have failed to discover other considerations relevant to this decision and thus what might count as reasons. We can now develop this idea of embedded critical practice further.

# Critical development

Critical practice aligned with developing expertise as seen above could provide a more natural way to work with new and uncertain situations and thus lead to a development of a robust professionalism.

As we know, everyday social work deals with risk, complexity and contingency, and so:

- There will be range of 'solutions'.

- Things will change.

- Outcomes cannot be predicted with utter certainty.

- Values and assumptions may not be valid in the future.

- There will be many other perspectives on a situation.

Working with uncertainty, by allowing for contingency and checking up on how things are going, is more likely to lessen its threat and its ability to make us feel defensive. If we list the main areas associated with professional and experienced practice (as seen above), we can align the necessary critical thinking activities which allow us to work positively with uncertainty (see Table 5.1). These activities will employ the intellectual resources of background knowledge, critical concepts, standards, principles and strategies we explored earlier in Chapter 1, and practice values should ensure the necessary habits of mind are inherently present.

**Table 5.1** Elements and activities of critical 'expert' practice

| Experience | Critical thinking activities |
|---|---|
| Awareness, control and evaluation of thinking processes | Thinking about thinking |
| Developing clusters of knowledge | Keeping up to date; reading<br>Integrating values and experience<br>Holding views based on valid evidence but seeking and accepting relevant but alternative viewpoints and perspectives<br>Identifying and challenging own and others' assumptions<br>Recognising and questioning viewpoints and arguments |
| Assessment of situations in depth<br>Selection and adaptation of 'schema' or framework that fits | Understanding when more information and input is required and knowing where and how to get it<br>Gaining alternative perspective/s or reframing a situation<br>Lateral/creative thinking; problem solving |

| Experience | Critical thinking activities |
|---|---|
| Leads to action | Decision-making and planning; use of discretion; responsibility; risk assessment<br>Seeking out and taking proper account of all stakeholders' input<br>Thinking through implications<br>Predicting possible outcomes, allowing for alternatives |
| Monitoring progress and evaluating outcomes | Formulating clear aims/objectives at start, getting feedback and making judgements<br>Being prepared to adapt, change and learn when necessary. |

This is what we call taking a 'critical stance' and becoming a 'critical practitioner' – it just means taking account of a less than perfect world whenever we can.

# Evidence-informed practice

There is a large amount of debate concerning 'evidence-informed practice' and its place within social work. It is not within the remit of this handbook to explore the arguments further and we have already looked at the critical use of literature for our purposes. As students within an academic environment you will be expected to gain an understanding of the current theory, research focus and policy development within your PQSW specialism and discuss such issues in your assignments. As professionals we have already seen that new knowledge and ideas enhance and develop practice expertise, but your depth of involvement with different types of research material will depend on various issues, for example:

- the emphasis of your work within a medical model (which is highly evidence-based);
- the research culture of your organisation.

As we have also seen, to apply or base practice on any type of evidence without moral or ethical sensitivity, a wider assessment of the context, individual circumstances and situational requirements or a risk assessment of possible implications would be deemed 'uncritical' practice and is unacceptable.

## *Review*

We do not have to pretend we are in a perfect world and always able to do the right thing. What we need to show and provide evidence for it is how we take account of the uncertainty and complexity of our role and how we try to work from a critical stance. Thinking critically must not be about feeling threatened or being made to feel inadequate. It is a holistic and positive way of approaching the world, and a natural one:

> *In as far as 'critical skills' go, learn to notice hunches, intuitions, gut feelings, the 'critique' is 'in there'.*

(Stokoe, 2003)

An awareness and acceptance of uncertainty in the practice of any professional is an important way to lessen stress. There are no perfect solutions out there to find, so we cannot be called on to work perfectly. If we accept the fact that the things we do or decide on are still dependent on something uncertain or on future happenings, and work in a way that takes account of that (i.e. constantly reviewing the things we deal with, decide on or do), then this is really what 'thinking critically' is all about.

*FURTHER READING*

**Adams, R., Dominelli, L. and Payne, M.,** (eds) (2002). *Critical practice in social work*. Basingstoke: Palgrave.

**O'Sullivan, T.** (1999) *Decision making in social work*. Basingstoke: Macmillan.

# *Chapter 6*
## Summary

As we have seen, our original set of intellectual resources for critical thinking can be applied to all areas of the PQSW Programme and be aligned with PQSW activities such as critical reflection, reflective learning and critical writing. It comes down to three basic abilities – questioning, analysing and evaluating – which dovetail into the various methods associated with professional practice as well as learning.

Critical reflection can enable the identification, exploration and understanding of practice activities, e.g. decision-making, managing risk, exercising power and responsibility, using discretion, integrating values. Reflective learning will enable these activities to develop with new knowledge and new experiences. Writing critically allows an appropriate academic structuring and evidencing of this reflection for assignments, and enables a more thorough critical analysis and evaluation of the knowledge being acquired and the learning taking place.

This whole process can also constructively move our practice forward to incorporate any necessary change and development. In this way, practice knowledge is developed further for ourselves, for others and for the profession itself as we begin to develop and articulate our own practice theories, constantly evaluated in the light of new experience and knowledge. More holistically, it develops a way of being as a practitioner.

We may not have a lot of time for critical thinking, reflection or writing and, as abilities or qualities, they are processes that need experience and practice in order to be learnt effectively. The PQSW award provides the opportunities for the experience and practice, and also gives you the credit for doing it. The other good news is that you can develop your abilities by being aware of and understanding the various elements involved and by having some methods to follow. In this respect we hope this handbook has given you a better understanding, as well as some useful ideas to work with.

Finally, good thinking, reflecting and writing skills help you to deliver good social work, as you become more able to develop and articulate the resources and services for your service users and be accountable for them. We hope that throughout all your efforts in developing 'critical thinking' your service users will benefit.

# *Appendix*
## The Harvard Referencing System

The following brief guidance is based on the system that Bournemouth University uses and our experience. Please refer to your own institution's regulations.

Bournemouth University, like many universities, uses the Harvard Referencing System as advised in the following British Standards:

- BS 5605:1990. Recommendations for citing and referencing published material, 2nd edn. London: BSI.

- BS 1629:1989. Recommendations for references to published materials. London: BSI.

References are cited in two different places. Firstly at the point at which a source is referred to in the text of the work; secondly in a list at the end of the work – the reference list.

The following examples are all fictitious and any resemblance to existing works is purely coincidental.

## Citing in the text

The Harvard system is also called the author/date method because sources are referred to in the text by giving the author's surname and the year of publication. For citations referring to particular parts of the document the page number may be given after the year. For example:

- Smith (2005) showed us the importance of referencing in academic work…

- The five particular ways in which referencing affects academic work have been clearly explored by Smith (2005, p. 24)…

- Referencing is very important in academic work (Smith, 2005)…

*Tip*: Many people find it difficult to remember where the brackets go. A simple tip is to consider whether the author's name forms part of the text. In our first two examples above, the name Smith forms part of the sentence, so it is not put in the brackets (only the date). In the third example, the name Smith does not form part of the sentence, thus the author's name goes in the brackets with the date (Smith, 2005).

### Problems

- No author?
  - The author (i.e. the originator) may be the organisation shown most prominently in the source as responsible for the content in its published form.
  - For certain kinds of work, e.g. dictionaries or encyclopaedias, or if an item is the co-operative work of many individuals, none of whom have a dominant role, e.g. videos or films, the title may be used instead of an originator or author.
  - For completely anonymous works, use 'Anon.' instead of a name.
- No date?
  - If an exact year or date is not known, an approximate date preceded by '*ca.*' may be given in square brackets , e.g. [*ca.*1750].
  - If you can't make an approximate date then you state 'no date' in square brackets, i.e. [no date].

# Reference List

At the end of the work the references are listed in alphabetical order of originator's surnames.

*NB*: A bibliography is a list of all works that have influenced the writer of the text, not just the ones directly referred to. You will usually be asked for a reference list rather than a bibliography.

### Problem

- The same author is being listed more than once
  - If you have cited more than one item by a specific author they should be listed chronologically (earliest first), and by letter (2001a, 2001b) if the author has published more than one work in a specific year.

The elements of a reference need to be in a specific order. Here are just a few (fictitious) examples:

## Books

AUTHOR/ORIGINATOR (surname and then initials),
Year of publication.
*Title*.
Edition (if not the first).
Place of publication:
Publisher.

e.g.   SMITH, B., (2005). *How to reference*. London: Bloggs Publishing.

*Problems*

- The book chapter has a different author
  - You make the chapter author the main originator and give the title of the chapter and its pages as well, as follows:

    JONES, J. R., (2005). Citation and plagiarism. In: B. Smith, ed. *How to reference*. London: Bloggs Publishing, pp. 502–10.

- The person you are referencing is being quoted in another work
- In the text you *must* cite both authors, e.g. as follows:

  A study by Harris and Keeble (1996, cited Smith, 2005, p.24) showed that...

  but only list the work you have used, i.e. Smith, in the reference list at the end of your work.

## Journals

AUTHOR/ORIGINATOR (surname and then initials),
Year of publication.
Title of article.
*Title of journal*,
Volume number and (part number),
Page numbers of contribution.

e.g.   SMITH, B., (2004). The referencing nightmare.
        *Journal of Referencing and Citation*, 9 (1), 28–41.

## Websites

AUTHOR/ORIGINATOR (surname and then initials),
Year.
*Title* [online].
Place of publication: Publisher (if ascertainable).
Available from: URL [accessed date].

e.g.   SMITH REFERENCING COMPANY, (2003). *Referencing guidelines* [online]. London: Smith Referencing Co. Available from: http://www.smithreferencing.co.uk [accessed 23 Oct. 2004].

# Bibliography

**Adams, R., Dominelli, L. and Payne, M.** (eds) (2002) *Critical practice in social work*. Basingstoke: Palgrave.

**Alter, C. and Egan, M.** (1997) Logic modeling: a tool for teaching critical thinking in social work practice. *Journal of Social Work Education*, 33 (1): 85–103.

**Argyris, C. and Schön, D.** (1974) *Theory in practice: increasing professional effectiveness*. San Francisco, CA: Jossey-Bass.

**Bailin, S., Case, R., Coombs, J.R. and Daniels, L.B.** (1999) Conceptualising critical thinking. *Journal of Curriculum Studie*s, 31 (3): 285–302.

**Barnett, R.** (1997) *Higher education: a critical business*. Buckingham: Society for Research in Higher Education and Open University Press.

**Baxter Magolda, M.** (1992) *Knowing and reasoning in college*. San Franciso, CA: Jossey-Bass.

**Bloom, B.S. Jr** (1956) *Taxonomy of educational objectives: handbook 1. The cognitive domain*. New York: McKay.

**Boud, D., Keogh, R. and Walker, D.** (1985) *Reflection: turning experience into learning*. London: Kogan Page.

**Bowlby, J.** (1951) *Maternal care and mental health*. Report to the World Health Organisation. New York: Shocken Books.

**Bowlby, J.** (1969) *Attachment and loss: attachment*. New York: Basic Books.

**Brockbank, A. and McGill, I.** (1998) *Facilitating reflective learning in higher education*. Buckingham: Society for Research into Higher Education and Open University Press.

**Brookfield, S.** (1987) *Developing critical thinkers*. Buckingham: Open University Press.

**Brown, R.B. and McCartney, S.** (2002) Multiple mirrors: reflecting on reflections. In R. Adams, L. Dominelli and M. Payne (eds), *Critical practice in social work*. Basingstoke: Palgrave, pp16–31.

**Burgess, R.C.** (1999) Reflective practice: action learning sets for managers in social work. *Social Work Education*, 18 (3): 257–70.

**Center for Critical Thinking** (2003) *Improve thinking on and off the job* [online]. USA: Critical Thinking Consortium. [Accessed 19 October 2003.]

**Coleman, H., Rogers, G. and King, J.** (2002) Using portfolios to stimulate critical thinking in social work education. *Social Work Education*, 21 (5): 583–95.

**Cottrell, S.** (2003) *The study skills handbook*. Basingstoke: Palgrave Macmillan.

**Curry, L. and Wengin, J.F.** (1993) *Educating the professional*. San Fransisco, CA: Jossey-Bass.

**Eraut, M.** (1994) *Developing professional knowledge and competence*. London: Routledge.

**Fisher, A.** (2001) *Critical thinking. An introduction*. Cambridge: Cambridge University Press.

**Fisher, T. and Somerton, J.** (2000) Reflection on action: the process of helping social workers to develop their use of theory in practice. *Social Work Education*, 19 (4): 387–401.

**Ford, P., Johnston, B., Mitchell, R. and Myles, F.** (2004) Social work education and criticality: some thoughts from research. *Social Work Education*, 23 (2): 185–98.

**Ford, P., Johnston, B., Mitchell, R. and Myles, F.** (2005) Practice learning and the development of students as critical practitioners: some findings from research. *Social Work Education*, 24 (4): 391–407.

**Ghaye, A. and Ghaye, K.** (1998) *Teaching and learning through critical reflective practice*. London: David Fulton.

**Gibbs, L. and Gambrill, E.** (1999) *Critical thinking for social worker: exercises for the helping profession*. London: Sage.

**Gibbs, L. and Gambrill, E.** (2002) Evidence-based practice: counter arguments to objections. *Research on Social Work Practice*, 12 (3): 452–76.

**Gould, N. and Taylor, I.** (eds) (1996) *Reflective learning for social work*. London: Arena.

**Halonen, J.S.** (1985) Demistifying critical thinking. *Teaching Psychology*, 22 (1): 75–81.

**Hamill, C.** (1999) Academic essay writing in the first person: a guide for undergraduates. *Nursing Standard*, 13 (44): 38–40.

**Ixer, G.** (1999) There's no such thing as reflection. *British Journal of Social Work*, 29: 513–27.

**Johns, C.** (2000) *Becoming a reflective practitioner*. Oxford: Blackwell.

**Kolb, D.A.** (1984) *Experiential learning. Experience as the source of learning and development*. Englewood Cliffs, NJ: Prentice Hall.

**Macauley, C.** (2000) Transfer of learning. In V.E. Cree and C. Macaulay (eds), *Transfer of learning in professional and vocational learning*. London: Routledge, pp1–26.

**Maslin-Prothero, S.** (ed.) (2001) *Baillière's study skills for nurses*, 2nd edn. London: Baillière Tindall and RCN.

**Maudsley, G. and Scrivens, J.** (2000) Professional knowledge, experiential learning and critical thinking. *Medical Education*, 34: 535–44.

**Mezirow, J.** (1981) A critical theory of adult learning and education. *Adult Education*, 32 (1): 3–24.

**Mezirow, J. and associates** (eds) (1990) *Fostering critical reflection in adulthood. A guide to transformative and emancipatory learning*. San Fransisco, CA: Jossey-Bass.

**Moon, J.** (1999a) *Learning journals: a handbook for academics, students and professional development*. London: Kogan Page.

**Moon, J.** (1999b) *Reflection in learning and professional development: theory and practice*. London: Kogan Page.

**Moon, J.** (2004) *A handbook of reflective and experiential learning. Theory and practice*. London: RoutledgeFalmer.

**Mumm, A.M.** (1997) Teaching critical thinking in social work practice courses. *Journal of Social Work Education*, 33 (1): 75–85.

**Newman, T.C.** (2000) *Developing evidence-based practice in social care: locating, appraising and using research findings on effectiveness. Guidelines for practitioners.* Exeter: CEBSS.

**O'Reilly, D., Cunningham, L. and Lester, S.** (eds) (1999) *Developing the capable practitioner.* London: Kogan Page.

**O'Sullivan, T.** (1999) *Decision-making in social work.* Basingstoke: Macmillan.

**Parker, J.** (2004) *Effective practice learning in social work.* Exeter: Learning Matters.

**Philips, V. and Bond, C.** (2004) Undergraduates' experiences of critical thinking. *Higher Education Research and Development,* 23 (3): 276–94.

**Plath, D., English, B., Connors, L. and Beveridge, A.** (1999) Evaluating the outcomes of intensive critical thinking instruction for social work students. *Social Work Education,* 18 (2): 207–17.

**QAA** (2001) *The framework for higher education qualifications in England, Wales and Northern Ireland – January 2001* [online].Gloucester: The Quality Assurance Agency for Higher Education Available from: http://www.qaa.ac.uk/academicinfrastructure/FHEQ/EWNI/default.asp#framework. [Accessed January 2005.]

**Race, P.** (2001) *The lecturer's toolkit,* 2nd edn. London: Kogan Page.

**Rolfe, G., Freshwater, D. and Jasper, M.** (2001) *Critical reflection for nursing and the helping professions. A user's guide.* Basingstoke: Palgrave.

**Saltiel, D.** (2003) Teaching reflective research and practice on a Post Qualifying Child Care programme. *Social Work Education,* 22 (1): 105–11.

**Schön, D.** (1983) *The reflective practitioner: how professionals think in action.* London: Temple Smith.

**Schön, D.** (1987) *Educating the reflective practitioner.* London: Temple Smith

**Secker, J.** (1993) *From theory to practice in social work. The development of social work students' practice.* Aldershot: Avebury.

**Sheldon, B. and Chilvers, R.** (2000) *Evidence-based social care. A study of prospects and problems.* Lyme Regis: Russell House.

**Smith, F.** (1992) *To think: in language, learning and education.* London: Routledge.

**Sotto, E.** (1994) *When teaching becomes learning: a theory and practice of teaching.* London: Continuum.

**Stokoe, L.** (2003) *Critical analysis skills* [online]. Worcester: University College Worcester. [Accessed 7 January 2004.]

**Van Manen, M.** (1995) On the epistemology of reflective practice. *Teachers and Teaching: Theory and Practice,* 1 (1): 33–50.

**Watson, F., Burrows, H. and Player, C.** (2002) *Integrating theory and practice in social work education.* London: Jessica Kingsley.

**Weick, A., Rapp, C., Sullivan, W.P. and Kristhardt, W.** (1989) A strengths perspective for social work practice. *Social Work,* 34: 350–4.

**Yelloly, M. and Henkel, M.** (eds) (1995) *Learning and teaching in social work: towards reflective practice.* London: Jessica Kingsley

# Index

Added to the page number 't' denotes a table.